# Spiritual & Comfo[illegible]
# Coloring Book



## This book belongs to

____________________________

## Date

____________________

Illustrated by Katerina Grik

Obsessed with the coloring pages in this book?

Thank you for your Amazon review and supporting Blik Books!

Enjoy 5 FREE exclusive coloring pages as our token of appreciation!

Simply DM @BLIKBOOKS on Instagram and drop your email to

receive your complimentary PDF!

# Color Testing Pages

# WRITE DOWN YOUR MOST BEAUTIFUL MEMORIES AND TELL HOW YOU FEEL NOW

To live in hearts we leave behind is
not to die

If light is in your heart, you
will find your way home

As the seasons change, the
love we shared remains
constant. It is a beacon of
light that guides me through
the darkest nights of grief

Your love continues to be a guiding force

As you navigate this
challenging path, please remember
that you are not alone

There are no goodbyes for us...
Wherever you are, you will always
be in my heart

# WRITE DOWN YOUR MOST BEAUTIFUL MEMORIES AND TELL HOW YOU FEEL NOW

You are a part of my yesterday,
my today, and my tomorrow.
Your love echoes in the chambers
of my heart, and I carry your
warmth with me, always

You are stronger than you know,
and brighter days await on the other
side of this storm

# WRITE DOWN YOUR MOST BEAUTIFUL MEMORIES AND TELL HOW YOU FEEL NOW

It's during these moments of profound loss
that the strength of your spirit shines through

May the love you shared continue to
echo in the chambers of your heart,
bringing solace and warmth

The pain passes, but the beauty remains

Reach out when you need to, and know that your pain is acknowledged and shared

Your laughter, your kindness,
and the warmth of your
presence are vivid memories

WRITE DOWN YOUR MOST BEAUTIFUL MEMORIES AND TELL HOW YOU FEEL NOW

Be patient with yourself, know that
progress, no matter how small, is an
achievement

The stars shine brightest in
the darkest night. May you
find glimpses of light in your
moments of deepest sorrow

# WRITE DOWN YOUR MOST BEAUTIFUL MEMORIES AND TELL HOW YOU FEEL NOW

I will always love you
with all my heart

Your tears may fall, but love's
echoes linger, bringing solace
to your soul

# WRITE DOWN YOUR MOST BEAUTIFUL MEMORIES AND TELL HOW YOU FEEL NOW

Your beloved's memory will
forever be etched in the
fabric of your life, a
testament to the love and
connection you shared

Grief can be the garden of compassion.
If you keep your heart open through
everything, your pain can become your
greatest ally in your life's search for love
and wisdom

Though the path of grief is long and
winding, the footprints of our shared
journey remain imprinted on my
heart. Your love lights the way

# WRITE DOWN YOUR MOST BEAUTIFUL MEMORIES AND TELL HOW YOU FEEL NOW

Until we meet again, know that
you are loved beyond measure, and
your memory is a balm to my
wounded heart

Those we love don't go away; they walk beside us every day. Unseen, unheard, but always near

# WRITE DOWN YOUR MOST BEAUTIFUL MEMORIES AND TELL HOW YOU FEEL NOW

Grief is a journey, not a destination.
As you walk this path, may you find
strength in each step and comfort in the
love that surrounds you

Allow yourself the space to grieve, and remember
that it's okay not to be okay

Let go of what was, accept what is and have faith in what will be

In the dance of memories, let the
steps of joy and laughter lead you,
even in the midst of grief

In the embrace of memories, find comfort for your heartache.

May you find healing in the warmth
of shared stories and the embrace of
those who care

Surround yourself with the love and support of those
who understand the depth of your pain

I'll see you on the other side
of the stars

# WRITE DOWN YOUR MOST BEAUTIFUL MEMORIES AND TELL HOW YOU FEEL NOW

In the garden of memories, your
presence blooms eternally

When someone is in your heart, they're
never truly gone

Grief is like the ocean;
it comes on waves
ebbing and flowing

WRITE DOWN YOUR MOST BEAUTIFUL MEMORIES AND TELL HOW YOU FEEL NOW

Though it may feel like the night is
endless, remember that the dawn is
just beyond the horizon

Your tears are the rain that nourishes the seeds of healing within.

May your heart find comfort in the gentle showers of love.

Illustrated by Katerina Grik

Made in the USA
Las Vegas, NV
31 March 2024